Balancing the Energy Equation
One Step at a Time!

written by
Michelle Lombardo, D.C.

illustrated by
M.R. Herron

WELLNESS
INCORPORATED

Hi there! It's me again, Hardy Heart. As you may know, I'm the leader of The OrganWise Guys Club. I'm here today to talk about a subject that is near and dear to my heart. . . getting you kids MOVING!

This is the second part of the book we recently published called, *Pepto's Place, Where Every Serving Size is OrganWise.* Some of you may have already read it. If not, you can check it out after you read this one. Let me take a minute to tell you how these books came about. They both start out the same, but read on to see how they balance each other out!

Not too long ago, Sir Rebrum had been surfing the web, as usual. He is always telling us health facts he learns while surfing. What we had noticed over the past several months was that certain words came up over and over again. He kept referring to terms like *overweight*, *sedentary*, *chronic disease* and *obesity*. One day I asked him to put these words into simple terms that we could understand so we would know what in the world he was so concerned about.

That was all Sir Rebrum needed to hear. Within 24 hours he had us gathered around for our first lecture from the future researcher, Sir Rebrum, Ph.D

He began by talking about something called the CDC. He explained that it was short for The Centers for Disease Control and Prevention, which is an agency in the United States whose mission is to help keep Americans healthy. One of the things the CDC does is research health issues to see what types of trends are happening in our country. He then began showing us all kinds of charts and graphs to try to explain that Americans are on their way to becoming seriously overweight and unhealthy. We were having a difficult time understanding what all those charts and graphs meant. That's when I asked, "Hey, could you put this in terms that someone other than a brain can understand?"

Sir Rebrum simplified it like this: "It's all about balancing the food you eat with the physical activity you do. When you take calories in by eating food, they are stored in your body for energy. This energy is waiting to get used. Physical activity or even more simply, MOVING, is what burns up this energy!

This is the energy equation for healthy weight. If you are balancing your food (calories you eat) each day with your physical activity (calories you burn) each day, you will keep your weight the same. If you eat more calories than you burn though, you will gain weight for that day. If you keep doing that day after day, you will become overweight."

Moving Less

Eating More

"Over the past several decades, many people have become overweight in this country," Sir Rebrum continued. "They have become unbalanced by eating more calories than they burn up. Since the amount of physical activity a person is getting each day is less and less, people are not burning up as many calories (energy) from the food they eat each day. When you don't use the calories for energy, the body stores it as fat." Then Sir Rebrum asked us to come up with some of the reasons why we thought kids were less active today than they had been in years past. Before I show you our list, what do you think some of the reasons may be?

Here are some of the ideas we came up with:

LiST

Too much television
Playing too many video games
No parks
Sitting at the computer
Homework
Driven to places instead of walking
No sidewalks
Don't feel safe playing outside
No bike trails
Lying around talking on the phone

From this list, it was easy to see why Americans are no longer on the move! That's what **this** book is all about . . . helping to come up with ways to keep kids from falling into the habit of an unbalanced energy equation when it comes to the physical activity side of the equation. (The book, *Pepto's Place*, is all about the eating side of this equation so be sure to read that if you haven't already.) It may not seem like a big deal now, but a lifestyle of an unbalanced energy equation can lead to more than just a weight problem. Did you know that being overweight is linked to some other very serious problems like heart disease, stroke, and diabetes?

Calci M. Bone, Madame Muscle, Sir Rebrum and I decided to take on this project. We want to help kids increase their physical activity to balance their energy equation and, if necessary, help them lose weight by burning more calories than they eat.

The first thing we did was to take a good, long look at the list we made. We decided to divide the list into the two categories on the sheets below.

As you can probably tell, Sir Rebrum helped us come up with these categories. I don't think I would have even considered the term "environment." He explained to us that environment meant "our surroundings." But before I show you how we categorized them, take a moment and decide in which category you would put each item from the previous page.

We had some long discussions about a couple of the items because we felt some of these could go on both lists. So that's what we did with them. Check it out.

Things that kids have a personal choice about:

Too much television
Playing too many video games
Sitting at the computer
Homework
Driven to places instead of walking
Lying around talking on the phone

Things that needed changing in the environment:

No parks
Homework
Driven to places instead of walking
No side walks
Don't feel safe playing outside
No bike trails

As you can see, *homework* came up on both lists. This is because kids do have somewhat of a choice as to whether they want to do their homework or not <u>and</u> the school (environment) can decide how much homework a student is given. Well, Sir Rebrum threw his two cents in right away. He said when it came to homework, kids should do ALL of their required homework. There was no way he was going to support kids getting out of this! With him being a brain, I guess we could understand why a good education is so important to him! Actually we all had to agree with him on that one.

We also put *driven to places instead of walking* on both lists, too. Sometimes kids need to get rides to places since there are no sidewalks or safe ways for them to walk. So the environment needs changing by adding more sidewalks. On the other hand, a lot of times kids ask for rides down the block when they could just as easily walk or ride their bikes to get some physical activity!

This list was looking a little overwhelming. Calci suggested that we pick one of the categories to work on first. Since we love teaching kids about making healthy personal choices, it seemed a natural fit for us to focus on category one. We know changing the environment is a very important part of getting people more physically active, but we'll have to focus on that list at another time.

No one had noticed that during this discussion, Madame Muscle had taken over Sir Rebrum's usual spot at the computer.

"Hey, what are you doing over there?" asked Calci.

"I'm looking something up on a website," Madame Muscle answered. "The other day I came across a site about a program called, *America on the Move*. It's a program to help get people to walk more. It uses something called a pedometer to count the number of steps a person takes each day."

Well, Sir Rebrum was all over that. He loves gadgets. So he said, "Scoot over and let the master take control!" Needless to say, within 15 minutes, Sir Rebrum had all kinds of information on pedometers, walking research and walking programs.

"I say we test out a walking program for ourselves! Let's do our own little *pilot study* to see if these pedometers might be something that kids could use to keep track of their steps!" Sir Rebrum suggested.

And that is exactly what we did. The next morning, Sir Rebrum purchased four pedometers, one for each of us to wear. He said that normally kids wore these on the waistbands of their pants, skirt or belt. But with us being organs, we needed a little specially-made belt to keep ours on. Then he had each of us test our counters. First, we needed to make sure the cover was closed.

Then we each counted out 100 steps as we walked. We checked our counters. As long as they read between 90 and 110 they were considered accurate. All of ours were within that range. We were ready for the experiment.

Sir Rebrum handed each of us his newly designed, "The OrganWise Guys Step Counting Book." (Someone had a busy night last night!) During the first week, he wanted each of us to go about our normal daily activities. He didn't want us to change anything that we normally do. He wanted to see where we all were. He called it our *baseline.* I guess if we were doing a *pilot study* we needed to use scientific terms! At the end of the day, before we went to bed, we were to record our steps for the day in the steps column. We all planned to meet first thing the next day and take a look at how we did. Sir Rebrum also reminded us to put our pedometers on first thing each morning and reset it to zero for the new day.)

And that's what we did. We each came back the next day with our steps recorded. I had 8,100 steps, Calci (as you can see below) had 4,502 steps, Madame Muscle had 10,007 steps and Sir Rebrum had 5,900 steps. Wow, we were all impressed with Madame Muscle!

"So what does all of this mean?" we asked.

"How far did we really walk?" I asked.

I figured you would want to know the miles," said Sir Rebrum. (That's what we all wanted to know . . . exactly how far we had "stepped" in miles.) "So I came up with a little graphic chart (I even used you guys in it!) so you can look up your steps and find out the approximate number of miles you walk each day. One mile is right around 2,000 steps. So every time you walk 2,000 steps, you are walking a full mile!" he continued.

I broke the chart down into half-mile increments. It's not as hard as it sounds. You all have this chart on the back cover of your *Step Counting Book*," Sir Rebrum finished.

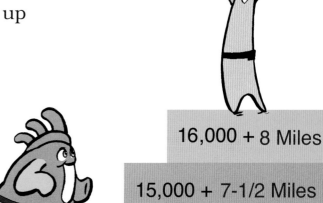

16,000 +   8 Miles

15,000 +   7-1/2 Miles

14,000 +   7 Miles

13,000 +   6-1/2 Miles

12,000 +   6 miles

11,000 +   5-1/2 Miles

10,000 +   5 miles

9000 +   4-1/2 miles

8,000 +   4 Miles

7,000 +   3-1/2 Miles

6,000 +   3 Miles

5,000 +   2-1/2 Miles

4,000 +   2 miles

3,000 +   1-1/2 miles

2,000 +   1 mile

We each looked up our steps to see how many miles we walked for the day. Check it out.

First I looked up my mileage of 8,100 steps. That makes it up to the 8,000 + step. Can you see where it falls? So that means I walked approximately four miles yesterday. Hey, that was pretty good, huh?

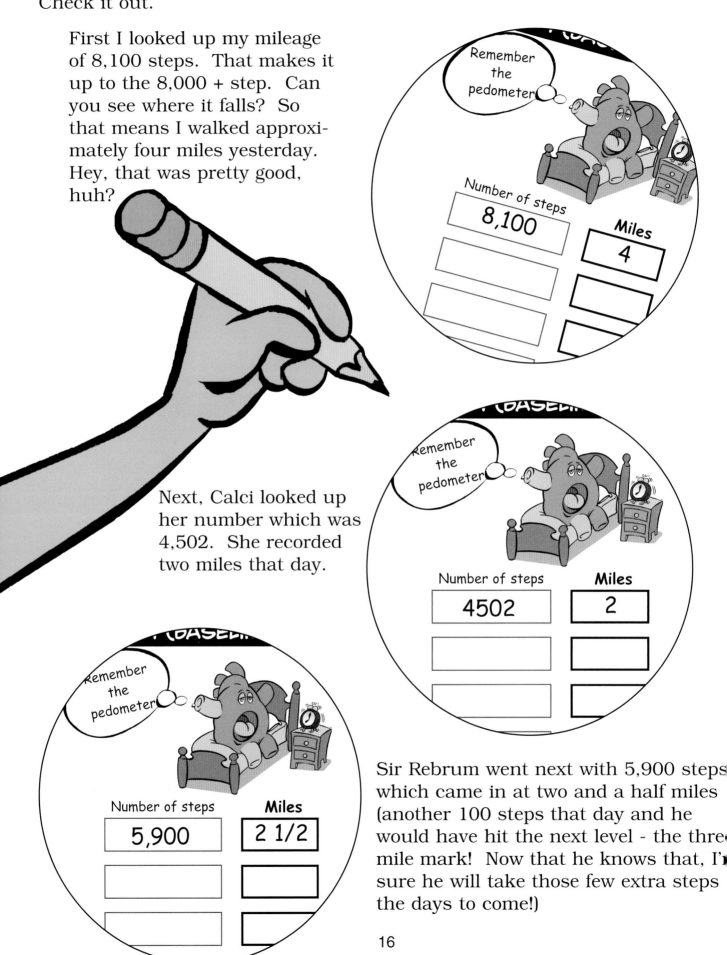

Remember the pedometer

Number of steps
8,100

Miles
4

Next, Calci looked up her number which was 4,502. She recorded two miles that day.

Remember the pedometer

Number of steps
4502

Miles
2

Remember the pedometer

Number of steps
5,900

Miles
2 1/2

Sir Rebrum went next with 5,900 steps which came in at two and a half miles (another 100 steps that day and he would have hit the next level - the three mile mark! Now that he knows that, I'm sure he will take those few extra steps the days to come!)

We saved the farthest for last! Madame Muscle's 10,007 steps came in at a whopping five miles! I guess since she's a muscle, she knows how important physical activity is. She said she has been doing a lot of walking for years.

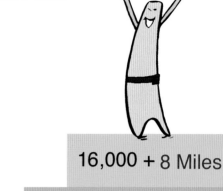

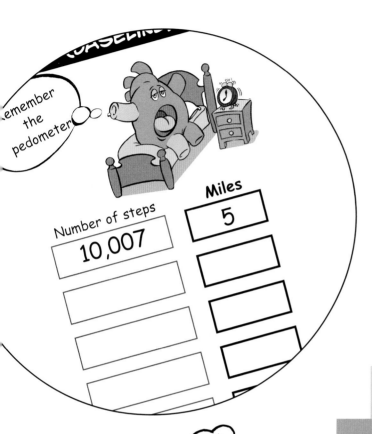

Remember the pedometer

Number of steps
10,007

Miles
5

16,000 + 8 Miles

15,000 + 7-1/2 Miles

14,000 + 7 Miles

13,000 + 6-1/2 Miles

12,000 + 6 miles

11,000 + 5-1/2 Miles

10,000 + 5 miles

9000 + 4-1/2 miles

8,000 + 4 Miles

7,000 + 3-1/2 Miles

6,000 + 3 Miles

5,000 + 2-1/2 Miles

4,000 + 2 miles

3,000 + 1-1/2 miles

2,000 + 1 mile

So, that week we all wore our pedometers, recorded our steps and figured out how many miles we walked each day. At the end of the week, we added up our total miles. It was very interesting to know how far each of us had walked.

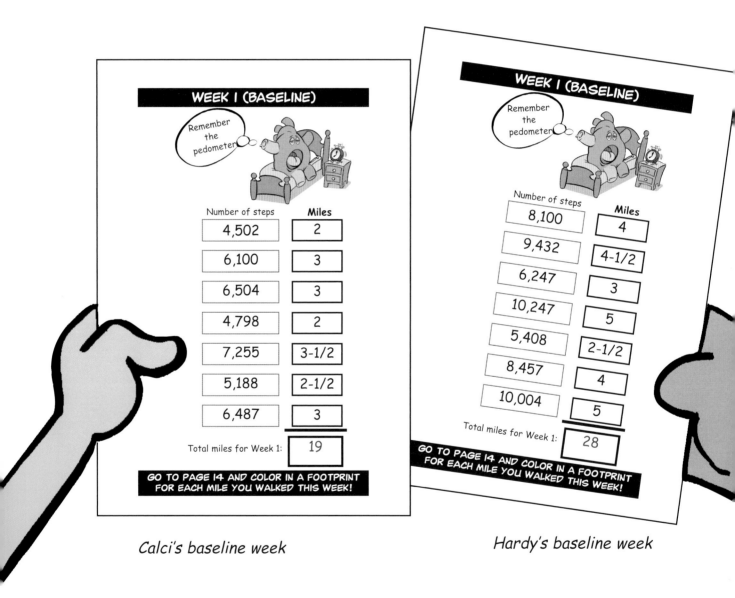

Calci's baseline week

Hardy's baseline week

And just to make it a little more fun, Sir Rebrum put a chart of footprints in the back of the book for us to fill in. We recorded the total number of miles we had walked each week by coloring in one footprint for every mile we walked.

Now we all knew where we stood when it came to our weekly mileage. For the next ten weeks, we were going to set goals and try to increase our miles each week. Sir Rebrum said he was very proud of each of us for the great habits we had formed during the *baseline* week. We were all in the good health habit of wearing our pedometers and recording our steps. We were off to a great start!

We were all really excited about this project, that is except for Calci. "What's wrong, Calci?" Madame Muscle asked.

"I'm a bone and I know how important exercise is and I seem to have the least amount of miles for the week," replied Calci. "I guess I need some help in getting motivated to move more."

"I'll help you," said the walking queen, Madame Muscle. "I'll spend a couple of days with you to show you all the little tricks I do to get in a lot of steps. You'll be surprised how quickly they add up!"

Sir Rebrum told us all to set a goal for the upcoming week. He said to be reasonable. He suggested trying to increase the mileage by at least five miles more than the total we walked during our *baseline* week. (I love using scientific, technical terms like *baseline*. Just call me Sir Rebrum!) We all set a goal and wrote it in the *Weekly Goal* box at the top of the page for the new week. Calci set her goal for 25 miles.

The next morning, as soon as Calci finished her breakfast, the door bell rang. It was Madame Muscle telling her that she would walk with her to school instead of getting a ride. After all, it was only a few blocks away.

During class, any time the teacher asked for a volunteer to do something, Madame Muscle would nudge Calci to raise her hand. (Calci never noticed until now that Madame Muscle was usually the one who volunteered to help *and get her steps in.*) The teacher called on Calci three times to run errands for her. That totaled over 500 steps just for being a good helper!

During recess, instead of sitting at the playground talking with friends, Madame Muscle had Calci and all of her friends up and WALKING while they were talking. Nothing like logging another 2,000 steps while catching up with all her friends. That was another mile for the day!

In class each day, Calci's teacher does a program called TAKE 10!® For ten minutes, the entire class does physical activity while they do their school work. Today they were doing TAKE 10! with math. (And, as you may notice, we OrganWise Guys happen to be featured in TAKE 10!) What a creative way to learn and get in more steps! Now that Calci was wearing her step counter, she really could see what a smart idea this was!

After school, Calci told the mother who usually drives them home, that she was on a new program to help her stay strong and healthy. She told her that he would only need a ride if the weather was bad. The rest of the kids in the carpool said they would like to walk, too. Before Calci knew it, the whole carload had jumped out and was following her. (Calci was quite impressed with herself. Who would have guessed that within one day she would become a "walking role model," inspiring other kids!) They had a great time the whole way while logging more steps.

As usual, once she got home, she jumped onto instant messaging. (For goodness sake, she hadn't talked to her friends in over 10 minutes!) But this time, instead of sitting there waiting for the replies, she marched in place while at the computer.

Later, when she was on the phone, she paced the floor instead of lying on the sofa. This logging steps was easier than she thought once she put her mind to it. By the end of the day, she had logged just over 8,262 steps. She couldn't believe it. She had hit the four-mile step!

Walking 8,262 steps was a lot better than any of the days during her *baseline* week. Just before she went to bed that night, she sent Madame Muscle one last instant message which read, "Thanks so much for your little stepping tricks, they make logging steps a breeze! (I wrote it out correctly for this book but, of course, she wrote it in that shorthand instant messaging code all you kids use!)

For the next ten weeks we were on a mission. Each week we challenged ourselves by increasing our weekly mileage goals! We all did quite well. And I have to tell you, Madame Muscle was a really great teacher and great sport! The week Calci out-walked Madame Muscle by three miles was a little tough for Madame Muscle. (Especially since Calci kept bringing it up every five seconds!) I think it sparked a little *healthy* competition between the two of them, because the next week they were walking maniacs!

know one thing, this *pilot test* sure helped us! Even we OrganWise Guys sometimes need a little extra motivation by using a program like this. I'm sure it will work for you kids, too. I know that programs using nice gadgets like pedometers are usually only used with older kids, but I know kids your age can be just as responsible as older ones.

These pedometers are the way to go. What a great birthday present to ask for or to do as a school project. (It would be fun to have one class compete against another to see who could walk the farthest!) Sir Rebrum has also printed his *The OrganWise Guys Step Counting Book!* for you to use. Or you can use a small spiral notebook and make up your own step counting book. Either way will work and you will be well on your way to balancing out your energy equation by taking it one step at a time! Good luck and get stepping!

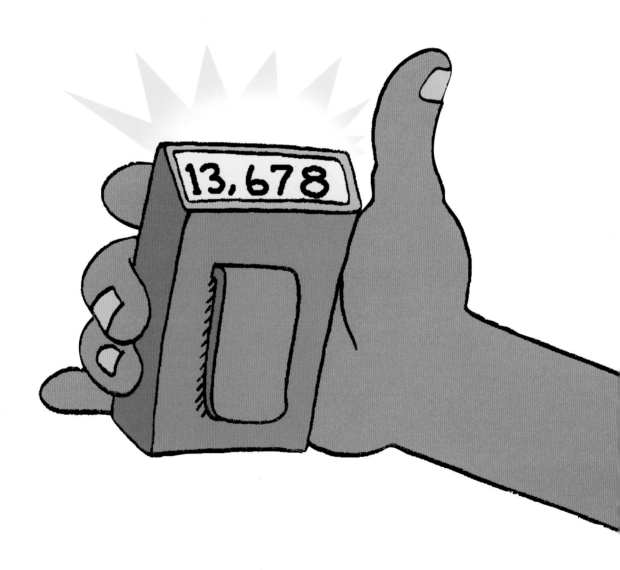

To find out more about ordering **The OrganWise Guys Step Counting Book**
visit www.organwiseguys.com or call 800-286-1730.

To find out more about the **America on the Move**™ program
visit www.americaonthemove.org

To find out more about the **TAKE 10!**® program visit www.take10.net